Moon Magic

Written and Illustrated by

Aurora Lightbringer

ISBN-10: 978-1976348341

ISBN-13: 197634834X

To Sorcia and Archer.
May the moon bestow
the brightest of
blessings upon you!

And to Wren, who is
growing up to be
quite a large
Nugget!

Look up in the sky and what do I see?

I see the moon shining down on me!

The waxing crescent

Curved and thin,

Means it's time to draw

Good energy in!

The waxing moon

Continues to grow,

Our hearts fill with hope

As we bask in its glow.

The full moon shines down

So round and bright,

Energy is strongest

On this magical night!

The moon starts waning

Begins to disappear,

As our hearts let go

Of worries, cares and fears.

The waning crescent

Like a thin letter "C",

Means it's time to release

Negative energy!

The dark moon rises

A time of rest and then,

The moon's magic cycle

Begins again!

A note from the Author...

Why honor the moon?

Great question! Across cultures and throughout time people have honored the moon. There are many calendars, events and celebrations that are dedicated to celebrating the moon and its cycles.

In everyday practice, following and honoring the cycle of the moon helps us to be more in touch with the cycles of nature and the cycles that exist in our own lives.

When we become more aware of the cycles that exist all around us, we can become more intentional about our place within them.

The following pages offer suggestions for everyday ways in which you can become more in tune with the moon and its cycles.

Everyday ways to honor the moon:

1. Make observing the moon part of your bedtime routine!
What phase is the moon in tonight?

2. Have a picnic in the moonlight!
What moon-shaped foods can you think of?

3. Take a moonlight hike!
This is especially magical in the snow!

4. Make moon bubbles!
Add a bit of sparkly powdered eyeshadow, glow-in-the-dark powder or fine-grain glitter to a bottle bubbles. You can add a few drops of essential oils like lavender, chamomile, patchouli, rose or lilac to the bubbles as well. On full moon nights, go outside and make wishes as you have fun blowing the moon bubbles (which will look like little full moons floating around).

5. Craft an evening yoga practice.
With the approval of a healthcare professional and under the guidance of a yoga instructor, craft a yoga practice that helps you wind down for the evening. You can try the poses featured in the illustrations of this book, adding an *asana* (pose) each moon phase until you have a full *vinyasa* (sequence) to practice in the moonlight.

Moon Prayers & Blessings

Use the space below to craft your own prayers/blessings to say during the different phases of the moon:

New Moon:

_____

_____

_____

Waxing Moon:

_____

_____

_____

Full Moon:

_____

_____

_____

Waning Moon:

_____

_____

_____

About the Author:

Aurora Lightbringer lives in Maryland where she enjoys painting, gardening and drumming by the campfire.

She is also an artist, teacher and mom.

To find out more, or to contact Aurora visit:
www.auroralightbringer.com

Merry meet and merry part and merry meet again!

Made in the USA
Lexington, KY
01 May 2019